I0568032

R.D. Talley Books Publishing, LLC
4882 W. Lone Mountain Rd.
Las Vegas, Nevada 89130
www.rdtalleybooks.com

Contents

Refuse to Lose

Multiple forces keep tugging at my flesh

trying to hold me back

& keep me from taking my next step

Whispering doubts in my ear

in hopes to keep me in fear,

taking all measures & chances

to prevent me from advancement…

But my genetics won't allow me to succumb,

my body refuses to stay numb,

my heart refuses to stop pumping,

my mind refuses to settle for nothing,

my skin is built too tough to liquidate,

my soul won't be affected from the hate,

God's light in me shines too bright

to give up on any fight for my life.

Pick-Up Rhymes (Pt. 1)

Beautiful…Queen…My Lady…

Your inner light can be seen from both within & without

even before a single word is released from your mouth

Your inner light attracts positive energy naturally,

so naturally, that when the moon comes out at night

it tends to focus on you, displaying you under a spotlight.

And I can't blame that moon for giving you

the much-deserved attention,

because I've lost count on all the things about you

that made me give my undivided attention

Please forgive me for my staring,

I don't mean to come-off as disrespectful

I've just never seen a woman's beauty

presented so radiantly & so bountiful

I know now for certain that God exists

because you are truly a miracle

In fact, I'm thanking Him now as I walk away

amazed at your beauty & how you remain humble.

R.I.P., Mr. Hussle

March 31st, 2019, approximately 3:20 pm

I was just leaving the book-signing of a fellow meaningful writer

feeling proud that I had supported another great artist

but soon felt a bit disturbed as my wife informed me

that close to that same area, we had lost another great artist…

At the time, I didn't know much about you Nip,

but it didn't take long before I realized that

2 more children will be moving-on without a father,

South Central L.A. had needlessly gained another martyr,

that you were a beacon of hope in your community,

and you were a light in the darkness of several other communities…

It puzzles me on why our culture insists

on continuing this vicious cycle of killing our own army

instead of supporting each other and realizing the many barriers

working against us & work to strengthen our cultural army…

but as of now our culture remains to be a laughing-stock for some other cultures.

I pray that you found Christ before you made your exit

so you could sit back in heaven and witness peacefully

as several of us artists work to continue your legacy

and make your dream become a reality.

From King to Queen

Dear Queens,

We all have come from you.

We are reflective images of you.

A lot of us were changed by the love of you.

Our support comes primarily from you.

So if we dare to call you out of your names,

then what does that make us?

If we treat you less than royalty,

then what is our worth?

Us kings thoroughly realize

that a lot of so-called men have dropped the ball

but know that those bad apples

don't represent or speak for us all

We see your struggles,

we see your pain,

we appreciate all that you do

just to keep us from going insane

Be patient with us Queens.

We're working hard to correct

the wrongdoings of irresponsible men.

Haiku Quartet

I've messed up badly
Who can save me, or free me?
Who can right this wrong?

Your love is too deep
I'm swallowed alive in it
yet I want to stay

Laying next to you
makes me forget my problems
How do you do it?

The violence must cease
we claim that we must bring change
yet we reject peace

Metaphorically Speaking

I am a Godly-crowned king

yet I acknowledge & respect other kings

I am a light that shines in dark places

reaching to people who feel lost, misplaced, & hatred

My wife's throne was made only for her

as she rules the queendom created for her

her love strengthens & weakens me simultaneously

yet she only intends to bring out the best in me

My skin consists of ruggedness

to prevent penetration from foolishness

yet it becomes silk to my queen's touch

sending my blood into a state of rush

My heart is made of Wolverine metal…

quick-healing and indestructible,

fearless, incorruptible,

yet it remains loving & touchable…

therefore, we will not falter.

Power

I've been told numerous times that I possess a powerful positive energy

I've been told that my presence alone can make friends out of my own enemies

I've been told that I've deserve all of the assets that I hold currently

but it's all by the grace of God, and my actions are from the Holy Spirit living in me

I've been recognized as man that possesses & spreads insightful wisdom like treasures

I've been told that I'm perfect despite my flaws & that I excel beyond any measure

I've been told by others that being in my presence is a delight & true pleasure

but these are results of God bringing me through & out multiple stormy weathers

I realize that I'm a man who holds wealth, love, charm, intelligence, and power

I also know that these are gifts from God, who was there for me during my darkest hours

trying to take the credit for my achievements & prevails would make me a coward

because it's by God's grace & unconditional love that I remain to be empowered.

Men's Appreciation

Shout-out to all the men who are working hard & handling their business

trying to reach & teach the younger men the importance of staying out of mischief

The men who get up & walk their kids to school, making sure they get there safely & on time

and then pick them up & help them with homework before their bedtime

The men who do their best to raise their kids in ways to build them a better future

and teach them there's much more to life than always sitting in front of a TV or computer

The men who work diligently to provide,

The men who uplift the woman who's by their side,

The men who choose to lead by being a positive example,

The men who build their houses on firm foundations & protect their castles,

The men who trust God to help guide their families,

The men who constantly display love & humility,

The men who don't lash-out & become detrimental

whenever we face tough situations & our burdens become heavy.

I see you all. I support you all. I commend you all.

It's an honor to be among you all.

Keep your heads up & God bless you all!!

Flashbacks (Pt. 2)

I think and reminisce about the times when I was a boy…

constantly getting into trouble,

angry & confused from a divorced household,

stealing food & video games,

starting fights at school,

low confidence & low self-esteem,

never applying myself fully in anything,

too ashamed to smile,

blaming myself for things

that were out of my control…

Now I've become a symbol of greatness

and look to lead by example

for those who are looking up to me…

I'm mentoring these young men & women

and praying they don't make the same mistakes I made,

I'm also talking to grown adults

telling them that God has forgiven all the mistakes they've made…

So y'all please pray for me

as I try to lead these people down the right street.

Signing-Off

I can't thank you enough for your support!!

One of the reasons I made this was to express my appreciation towards you all so I pray that you enjoyed reading this "mixtape" poetry book.

Your support has enabled me to continue carrying-out a mission in spreading God's love to people, especially the ones who are in extreme need of it.

I'm still building my brand of books but my next focus is to begin visiting inmates in prisons & juvenile centers. My next book will be titled "On The Battlefield" and I look to release it in 2020.

To stay updated on my events, giveaways, interviews, performance videos, release dates, etc., feel free to follow me on my social media pages and website listed below. In the meantime, God bless you!!

Instagram: @roderickthewriter

Facebook: Author Roderick D. Talley

YouTube: R.D. Talley Books Publishing

Website: www.rdtalleybooks.com

Feedback & Pics

My lovely bride helping me out at one my vending events.

I thank God for her every day.

6 likes

cjfunctional @roderickthewriter loved the book. "Love Avenues" is my favorite chapter. If you like poetry this is a great read!! #iread #bookworm #blackauthors

Support from another great author, Mr. Cleon Joseph.

I'm reading his book now & it's very insightful.

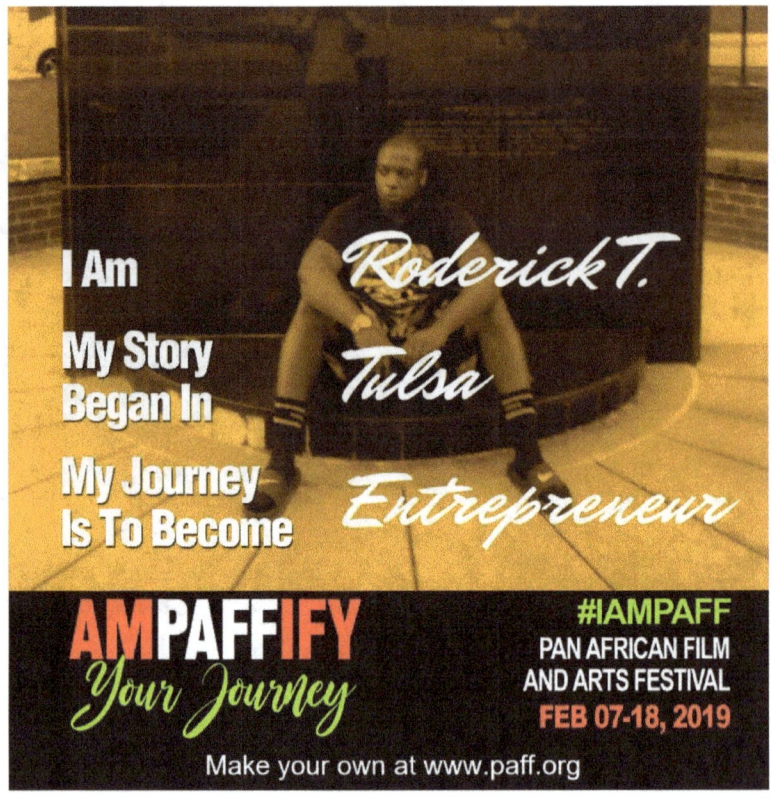

My first audition for a spoken word event.

I didn't make the cut but it was still a good experience.

One of the first times I was a featured artist at an event.

I pray that my words helped someone in that audience.

Receiving love & support from a fellow artist at a performing arts event.

3 likes

kyapublishing It was great to connect with #publishers R.D. TALLEY BOOKS this week here in Toronto, visiting all the way from Long Beach, California. Wishing them all the best with the new #publishingcompany, and happy we were able to meet in person!! P.S. Happy Anniversary!! 🇨🇦📚 #Repost @roderickthewriter

I'm big on networking & supporting other people who have positive purposes behind their work.

I'm looking forward to doing work in other cities down the road.

Toronto is definitely one of them so stay tuned if you live close to there.

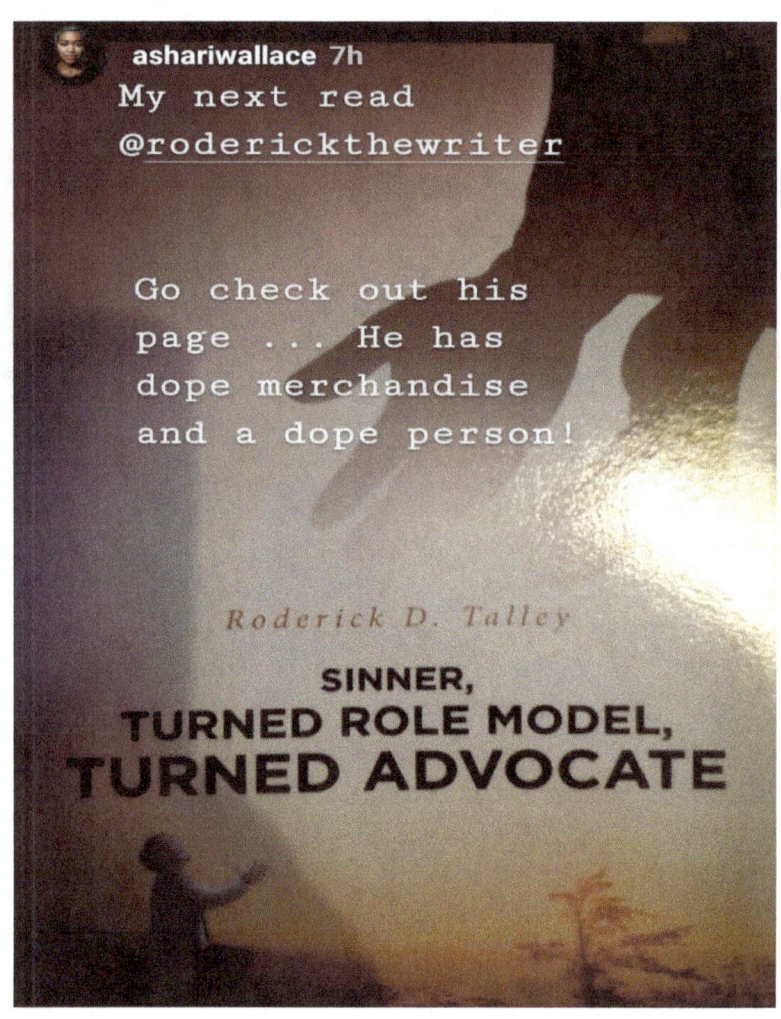

Another excellent author who's doing some very positive things.

God bless you, Ms. Wallace.

19 likes

songbirdeco I purchased my cousin's @roderickthewriter first book "Sinner turned Role Model turned Advocate". So excited to sit down and read it cover to cover. Woot Woot! Kudos Cuz!!!!

Family support. You got to love it.

Thank you, Jeff. God bless you cuzzo.

My first interview on a radio show.

Feel free to view it on my YouTube page

(R.D. Talley Books Publishing)

Hey man. Yeah I like your book. A few your poems I had to read a few times. Like flashbacks pt 1 and I'm not afraid. I actually had a dream not to long and it was deeeeeeep lol. So that one stuck out to me.

I havnt gotten to all of them just yet. But so far, u loving the vibe.

My biggest reward is knowing that I've encouraged & inspired people with my work.

Keep the feedback coming.

My dream of becoming an entrepreneur came to fruition just months ago. I'm still speechless. I have several great ideas for this company to help encourage and educate other people. One idea I have is having a spoken word tour in 2023 with a few other poets. Feel free to follow me on social media or visit my website www.rdtalleybooks.com for updates.